AF614923

Too Cute!

Baby Lions

by Elizabeth Neuenfeldt

BLASTOFF! Beginners

BELLWETHER MEDIA
MINNEAPOLIS, MN

Blastoff! Beginners are developed by literacy experts and educators to meet the needs of early readers. These engaging informational texts support young children as they begin reading about their world. Through simple language and high frequency words paired with crisp, colorful photos, Blastoff! Beginners launch young readers into the universe of independent reading.

Sight Words in This Book

a	have	see	with
at	look	some	
big	many	the	
eat	new	them	
find	other	they	
get	play	to	

This edition first published in 2024 by Bellwether Media, Inc.

Library of Congress Cataloging-in-Publication Data

Names: Neuenfeldt, Elizabeth, author.
Title: Baby lions / by Elizabeth Neuenfeldt.
Description: Minneapolis, MN : Bellwether Media, 2024. | Series: Blastoff! Beginners: Too Cute! | Includes bibliographical references and index. | Audience: Ages 4-7 | Audience: Grades K-1
Identifiers: LCCN 2023039883 (print) | LCCN 2023039884 (ebook) | ISBN 9798886877724 (library binding) | ISBN 9798886878660 (ebook)
Subjects: LCSH: Lion--Infancy--Juvenile literature.
Classification: LCC QL737.C23 N477 2024 (print) | LCC QL737.C23 (ebook) | DDC 599.757--dc23/eng/20230825
LC record available at https://lccn.loc.gov/2023039883
LC ebook record available at https://lccn.loc.gov/2023039884

Editor: Betsy Rathburn Designer: Jeffrey Kollock

Printed in the United States of America, North Mankato, MN.

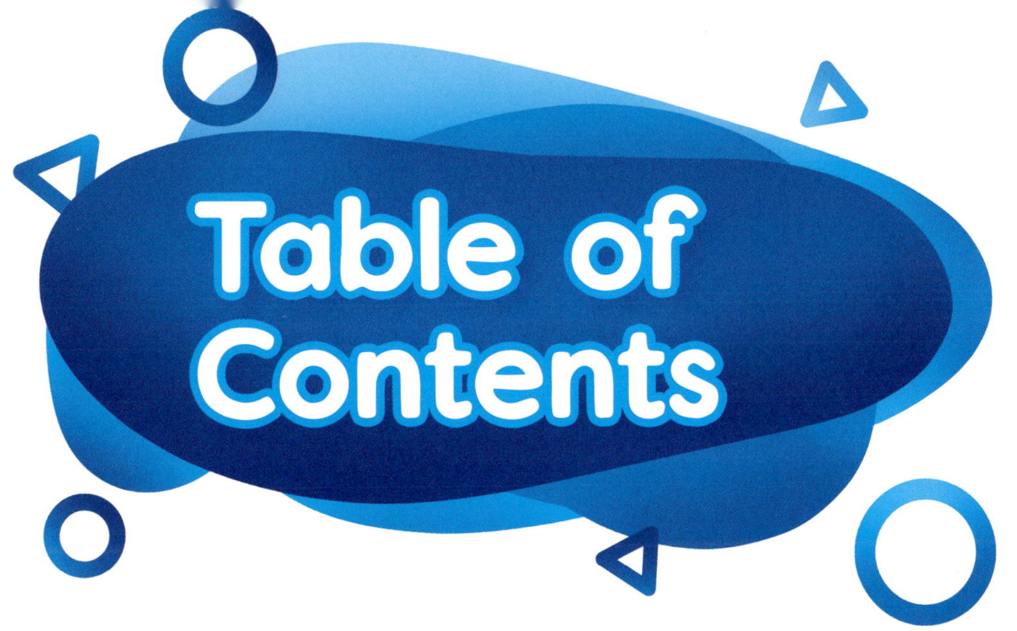
Table of Contents

A Baby Lion!

Look at the
baby lion.
Hello, cub!

Life in a Pride

Cubs have many **siblings**. They cuddle!

Newborn cubs sleep a lot. They cannot see.

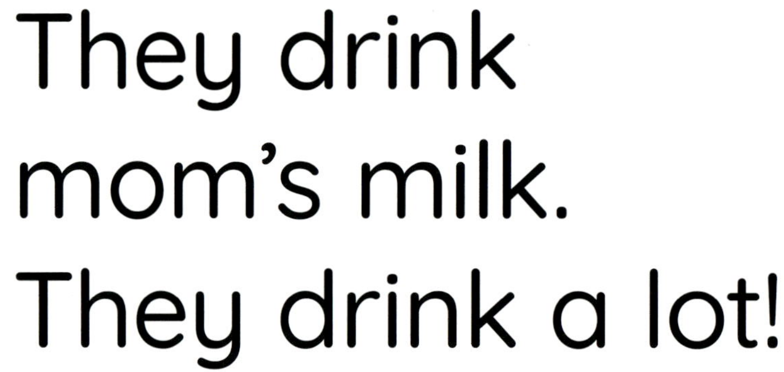

They drink
mom's milk.
They drink a lot!

drinking milk

mom

Cubs join mom's **pride**. They play with other cubs.

pride

Cubs stay clean! Mom **grooms** them.

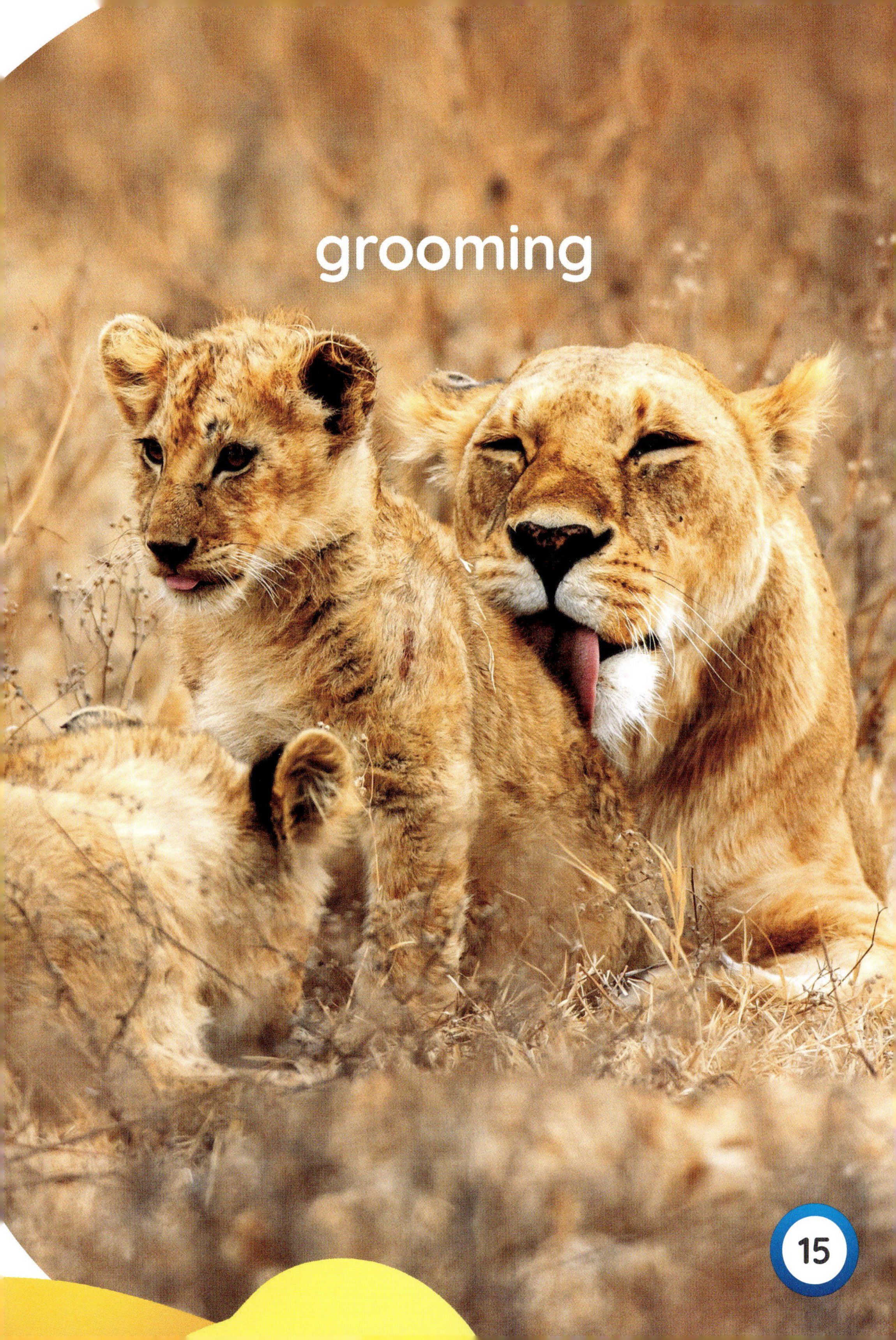

grooming

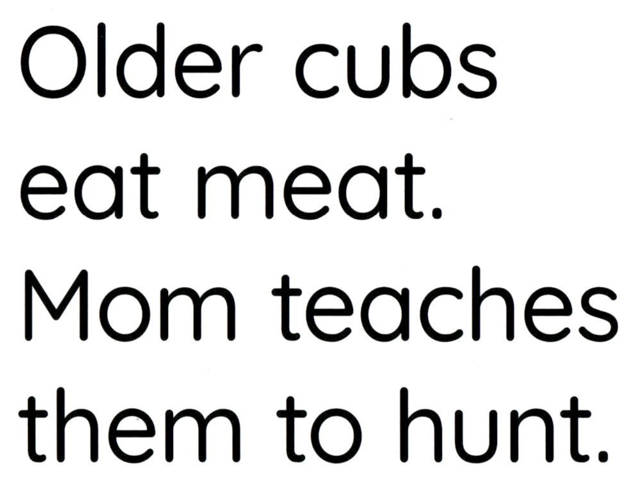

Older cubs eat meat. Mom teaches them to hunt.

hunting

Growing Up

Cubs get big!
Some cubs stay
with the pride.

Other cubs find a new pride. Bye, mom!

Baby Lion Facts

Lion Life Stages

newborn cub adult

A Day in the Life

sleep

play

hunt

Glossary

grooms

cleans

newborn

just born

pride

a group of lions that live together

siblings

brothers and sisters

To Learn More

ON THE WEB

FACTSURFER

Factsurfer.com gives you a safe, fun way to find more information.

1. Go to www.factsurfer.com.
2. Enter "baby lions" into the search box and click 🔍.
3. Select your book cover to see a list of related content.

Index

The images in this book are reproduced through the courtesy of: Eric Isselee, front cover, pp. 1, 3, 4, 5, 6, 22 (newborn, cub, adult); imageBROKER.com GmbH & Co. KG/ Alamy, p. 7; Wallenrock, p. 8; Laura Romin & Larry Dalton/ Alamy, p. 9; Design Pics Inc/ Alamy, p. 10; Holly Auchincloss, p. 11; JMx Images, p. 12; John Michael Vosloo, p. 13; zheng yaqi, p. 15; O'sokin, p. 17; Henk Bogaard, pp. 19, 22 (play); Amitrane, p. 21; Michaelsmart, p. 22 (sleep); Chris McLennan/ Alamy, p. 22 (hunt); Media Drum World/ Alamy, p. 23 (grooms); S.Tuengler - inafrica.de/ Alamy, p. 23 (newborn); Dagmara Ksandrova, p. 23 (pride); Dr Ajay Kumar Singh, p. 23 (siblings).